# Something New

Written by
**Marcia Vaughan**
Illustrated by
**Carol Way Wood**

ScottForesman

*A Division of* HarperCollins*Publishers*

Pup was tired of digging
holes.

"I want to do something new," said Pup.

3

"Spin with me,"
said Spider.

4

"Hop with me,"
said Hare.

6

"Skip with me,"
said Skunk.

8

"Pull with me,"
said Porcupine.

10

"Dash with me,"
said Deer.

"Wiggle with me," said Worm.

14